NOTES FOR A LIFE

Also by Sally Roberts Jones

Romford in the Nineteenth Century, 1969

Turning Away (poems), 1969

The Forgotten Country (poems), 1977

Elen and the Goblin, and other legends of Afan, 1977

Strangers and Brothers (radio poem), 1977

Books of Welsh Interest: an annotated bibliography, 1977

Allen Raine (Writers of Wales series), 1979

Relative Values (poems), 1985

The History of Port Talbot, 1991

Dic Penderyn: the Man and the Martyr, 1993

NOTES FOR A LIFE

New and Selected Poems
1953 - 2005

Sally Roberts Jones

HEADLAND

First published in 2010
by
HEADLAND PUBLICATIONS
Tŷ Coch, Galltegfa,
Llanfwrog, Ruthin,
Denbighshire LL15 2AR

Copyright © 2010 Sally Roberts Jones

British Library Cataloguing in Publication Data.
A full CIP record for this book is available from the British Library
ISBN: 978 1 902096 64 3

*All rights reserved. No part of this publication may be reproduced,
stored in a retrieval system, or transmitted in any form, or by any means,
electronic, mechanical, photocopying, recording or otherwise,
without the prior written permission of the publisher.*

*Requests to publish work from this book
must be sent to Headland Publications.*

*Sally Roberts Jones has asserted her right under Section 77 of the Copyright,
Designs and Patents Act 1988 to be identified as the author of this book.*

Printed in Great Britain by
Oriel Studios, Orrell Mount
Hawthorne Road
Merseyside L20 6NS

CONTENTS

Bangor Pier	9
Red Lion: Saturday, 1954	10
After the Camps	11
William Evans, Llangefni	12
Poet Reading	13
A Dressmaker in the Nineties	14
Good Intentions	15
Street Scene, Pilsen 1963	16
Five Views of Camden Town	17
To Daphni	19
Other Customs 1964	20
Professor X, Virginia	21
News of a Fire	22
The Dream	23
Reading John Clare	24
Moving House Again	25
Beginning	26
Talbot Memorial Park, Summer 1967	27
Rhossili	28
Hortus Inconclusus	29
Community	30
A Death in London, April 26th, 1972	31
The Antiquarian in the Countryside	32
Tea With Friends	33
Household Cavalry, Llansteffan	34
Sul y Blodau/Palm Sunday	35
Miscarriage	36

CONTENTS *continued*

After the Passion Play	37
The Apprentice Artist	38
Passing Acquaintance, Pontrhydyfen	39
A Stone for Remembrance	40
Enrolment Evening	41
Loss	42
Corsham Court Gardens, 1993	43
Random Thoughts of a Fallen Woman in Bute Street	44
Hawen Ward, The Infirmary	45
The Author Admits Guilt	46
Booklaunch, Southampton Row	47
Bingo	48
Scars	49
Waiting for the Funeral to Arrive	50
Found Poem	51
Flood Damage	52
Friends of Margam Park	53
Big Issue	54
Palm Saturday/Sadwrn y Blodau	55
Yugoslavia 1982	56
At the Dylan Thomas Centre	57
Acknowledgements	59

*For Huw, Owain, Gareth, Audrey and Cerys
with love*

BANGOR PIER

(For Luned)

Do you remember the heron
We saw that morning
Poised on the rocks; the thrush bearing
A snail shell, like a death's head warning ?

The long strolls on the broken pier
And the wind spying
About our legs with gusty leer,
Smelling of salt; the seaweed drying

On the rusty ladders and bars;
Tea tuppence cheaper,
But no stronger. There went the cars
On Beaumaris road; the pier keeper,

Like a revolutionary,
Was always knitting,
And we, never in a hurry
For all our work, were always sitting,

Talking, there in the old, cold hut,
And getting nowhere,
Like the boat we watched. that would cut
Back from the steps, into the shattered air.

RED LION: SATURDAY, 1954

(Homage to Caradoc)

This is the present pattern of the room,
Friezed glasses, wine-bright steel. Outside, the moon,
Carious with cloud, plucks up her net of leaves.

The stubble-crunching chatter moves along
To the next group; the tankards thud and bounce.
This is a privilege we have, to watch
These breathe: for thus

These are the damned, these living men who stand
In ever-changing line by foreknown hell;
These are the gods, self-damned, who, in their pews,
Drowsing, denounce their own well-hidden sins.

Tomorrow, Saturnalia forgotten,
They'll walk in bibled rows and curse our trade
With pious mouths and saintly hangovers.

AFTER THE CAMPS

(For Ethel Roberts, Llangefni 1955)

Making the beds, we talked of minor things,
Rain, and the lack of buses; just next door
Music turned up concealed fresh quarrellings;
Sunlight in netted patterns pooled the floor.

Oddly, we talked. Since time had made sense of sound
That man had confused. No horrors, of course;
Only the petty tyrannies, the round
Of minor afflictions -huge in their killing force.

Yet, was it this that maimed her -by dissent
Holding the cheapened flesh to dignity ?
Who now, by use and softness of consent
Is nothing as rare as heroines should be.

Only next door they murder while Lanza sings
Since, by her words, Death is in little things.

WILLIAM EVANS, LLANGEFNI

Often I saw him
Sweeping the empty streets,
Pushing his rusty barrow
Down the gutter.
We lured him with tea
Out of the harsh east wind
And he offered his store
In return for a friendly word.
He was nothing remarkable, though;
A little grey man
(His heart the conventional gold)
His thoughts as wholesome as bread
But without the yeast.

Yet at night, when the beer was flowing,
He knew his glory:
Verse ran from his eager lips
Faster than fire,
Till they gave him a bardic name
And crowned his wonder.
Brwshfab, Son of a Brush -
He knew that they mocked him
But knew that they had no malice:
He bore his title
Proud as a pencerdd down the dusty street.

I doubt if his tombstone bears it
Or tells his virtue:
Let this, then, honour his music
Who was our friend.

POET READING

(Jonathan Williams)

This is a poet,
A real live poet
(Though he reminds
Me of my father
Whose hair blew off in a thunderstorm
Twenty-five years ago
And never came back.)
However.
This is a poet,
Sounds like one,
Looks like one.
Out walking
You would not notice
He was a poet
Until you saw
He was the only
Ordinary man
In the street.

A DRESSMAKER IN THE NINETIES

Behind the shops the quiet squares unfold:
Adam, and Chippendale; and Lady Joan
Riding abroad each morning in the Row.
Elegance here, and decadence as well,
Fall with the fading leaves across the step,
Autumn of worlds that never came again.

Thus in one circle both the countries touch,
And Grandmother, walking quickly through the square,
Dreaming of what's to come, of spring and home,
Thinks that she moves in a city rare as gold
And sixty years later tells me this fairy tale
Of duchesses fitted, and queens in the early sun.

GOOD INTENTIONS

Cutting the trees, they cut the town away,
Drawing the sky between the ochre roofs;
Open a sudden gap where shadows were,
Baring the broken gutter, blistered paint.

Now you would think the trees could only die,
Lopped to a row of amputees, or grow
Crooked or cabbage-like if they survive;
Always the town must show its shabbiness,

Sunlight in summer find us as it will,
Householders note the damage, buy new paint,
Talk of the price of fencing. At weekends,
Watching the clouds, await the steady rain.

Slowly the trees expand; an autumn sun
Catches, too late, the surface of the leaves;
At Easter they'll cut the branches and the town
Shock us once more, diminished or decayed.

STREET SCENE, PILSEN 1963

They are queuing for bread just there;
Standing on cobbles, waiting.
And a tram goes by, and we shudder
"To think of having to queue --!"

Maps in a window, and pictures,
And a woman talking;
But I can't understand her; the pavements
Are black with an inch of dust.

Three soldiers with guns; some children
Asking for sweets:
Reporting the matter is simple.
But we don't understand.

FIVE VIEWS OF CAMDEN TOWN

1.
No ships in this Sargasso.
The current sweeps up
Paper and cabbage leaves,
Then the wind changes
And buffets away downhill,
Past the railway tracks.
And the wreckage is ankle-deep
Outside the Plaza.

2.
Come down in the world has Camden
But not in the market -
Seventeen junk-shops I counted in Maldon Road.
Stalls in a byway, fruit piled up by the gutter.
Crate upon crate -
What shall I buy you for Christmas ?
A secondhand bowler hat and a Chinese plate ?

3.
Caught suddenly sight of,
Rural by Primrose Hill,
The pastoral river:
Men fishing along the towpath,
A punt tied up at the steps
And a tree turning green.
All that it lacks is a milkmaid
And a suitably paintable cow.

4.
Browsing at bookstalls,
Always a fatal act
But this time rewarded
'Phra the Phoenician', gift-horse donated with soap,
Hides for me here.
One of the World's Best Books,
Its paper brittle and brown,
Key to a distant country, another's dream.

5.
Oh to be in Camden Town
When April's nearly here,
When pale skies wash the dusty stones
And wise men turn to beer.
No catkins in a budding grove
Or lambs across the fence:
Only a movement of the light,
A sixth and sharper sense.

TO DAPHNI

"Daphni remains one of the most splendidly Byzantine monuments
in Greece ... a series of mosaics without parallel ... In the dome
lowers the great Christ Pantocrator." (Fodor Guide)

Under the olive trees there were tents,
Laid out like a park; broad gravelled drives,
A banked stream, table-cloths hanging to dry,
Tables provided, rustic, incongruous.

That was the wrong place. Back on the road,
Trucks burning the road towards Corinth,
I might have been walking at home. The slopes
Were drier than dust, it felt
Like a used car lot, a back alley, a bomb site.

Only the road and the hills; the earth fell away
Before me; I passed a small church, the loose stones
Bit at my ankles, the shrubs were a forestry planting.
At last, turning back, I found it; the small church,
(Too small, surely, this ?) the cool courtyard, the two trees.

Inside, the mosaics sank back, the all-judging Christ
Was blinded. Red flowers on a balcony,
The pattern of bricks, echo of archway and dome,
Light cupped in the hands, a sacrament of the familiar.

I read in the guide-book - whatever they spoke of there
Existed no longer; the damaged face
Stared down, did not judge from appearance, was God.
Later, the words were still of another place,
The pictures too brazen: the miracle only art.

OTHER CUSTOMS 1964

Washington

In the hot evening, lugging a suitcase,
I was afraid.
Rough pavements,
Dustbins by broken steps,
The night dusty, velvety to the touch.
In an inhabited, empty square
The Public Library
Still open; who sat on the steps
I could not see, did not try to see.
Beyond it, children, playing the last game
Before bedtime.
A few groups on corners, a few cars
That, halting at cross-lights,
I carefully did not look at.
No reason for panic.
New in a foreign city,
Walking the little way to a waiting hotel;
The October night pleasant,
But the streets
More empty than seemed quite right;
Dark faces I did not look at
Avoiding mine.

Richmond

Even now, I cannot remember:
Suppose she must have been coloured,
But know she was older;
Holding the door, wondered at her confusion.
Only after we'd entered,
Seeing the segregation of the benches,
Knew it was not politeness here,
But challenge.

PROFESSOR X, VIRGINIA

The president of the Institute of Southern Culture
Has gravy stains on his front
And pretends to be
A wicked old man.

He tells us the children dream of Indians,
And is ambiguous about magnolias.
In the meantime,
Scalps a small handful of critics
Before the soup.

NEWS OF A FIRE

Waiting for you to be free
I wandered down
Past the hotel and courthouse.

Reindeer across the street
Were ready for Christmas,
Still more than a month away,

And a gramophone issued carols
Over the aisles of woolly vests,
Though the parakeets sang against them

And the tropic, unseasonal fish
Moved in the aerated waters
Under groves of dog-leads.

They have gone now, of course;
Rescued, perhaps, or promoted to glory in flames
With the phoenix, their fellow.

Yet because I have not seen them gone
And because
I was waiting for you, as I said,

There's something existing,
Idea of a bird or a fish,
That has not been consumed.

THE DREAM

In sleep the great house lies
In no known landscape.
The windows all face inwards.
I have seen it
Often: the hall, the portraits,
The desertion,
The fear that has no known object.

Mostly I find the attics,
Up some stairway
Broken, unsafe - sometimes a scaffolding
I climb with a terror
That will not relent.

Upstairs there's rubbish,
Furniture, old pictures -
A room that one might inhabit
If, in hunger,
Poverty gave no pride, cut off the will.

Spiders I loathe - so here there are no spiders,
Only the webs, thick, dusty, over all.
The attic has no ogres.
But something happens,
Always,
That is the essence of a fear.

What clues there are, escape;
I wake from dissolving panic,
But remember
Still that the mocking faces
Were not mine.

READING JOHN CLARE

(For my father)

You said you understood; his bitter voice
Spoke for you also. We, like shadows, moved,
Strangers, across the edges of your waste,
Further away than those you had not loved.

Once you set off by train -but that escape
Was always too easy, not the route desired.
Sometimes the aching nerves would prick a shape
Less than a man, a shambling beast retired

Out of all need to stand. We talked of God
(I prayed for a skill enough to answer you),
But none of it served. Yet time, that was his rod,
Worked for our wounds that cure long overdue.

You turned; in the light took up again your load
And walked for a day that cruel, sunlit road.

MOVING HOUSE AGAIN

I should be used to it now,
To all the circumstance,
The first shock of knowing,
And after, the slow destruction, the empty rooms.

Still, like the caddis fly,
I hoard stray ornaments,
The key from an altered lock,
A table-cloth,
Brass holders that lost their piano years ago.
After another or another move
These too will be left behind.

If love be evicted too,
By distance or death,
How long before memories,
Of no further use,
Are left in the empty room
With the old clock that does not go ?

BEGINNING

I can't see the stars;
Only a blackbird in the garden,
Singing his heart out in the rowan tree,
Sings to a rising moon.

Here I'm alone,
Not lonely for thinking of you,
Spinning a sort of dream
Without an end.

Blackbird and I,
Both in the springtime singing,
Singing for love,
For dreams, for the chance of spring

You, love, and I,
And the blackbird in the garden,
Drowned in the rowan tree
And the rising moon.

TALBOT MEMORIAL PARK, Summer 1967

This mediterranean sunlight pales the sky
To watered blue,
Makes shadows in the eye
Until the green
Grass of that turtle mountain
Shades away
Into the reddish strata of its shell.
Leaves shimmer, silver-gray,
Ash in the sun.

Not now, the statue says, we remember them:
In this drained summer
Sprawled on the charring turf
Where bronze and bandstand
Pin the park to earth.

In desert and plain the long campaigns begin:
An ant crawls on my hand,
The gardener
Waters his flowers with insecticide.

RHOSSILI

Tomorrow the tide will come at the proper time,
The sun burn hot on the rocks,
The clean sheep move
Idly across the path we do not walk.

Tomorrow -but now, today, the proper time
Curves into distance along the bay,
The gulls
Turn on the wind, slow as a stopping clock.

Wave after wave the pattern appears; we walk
Alone in a peopled land, no longer alone,
In a moment as long as our lives,
As short as a breath.

HORTUS INCONCLUSUS

In this garden
Daffodils and spring blossoms
Prepare a pastoral.

White walls
Stand in the sun; four socks
Two vests and a towel

Paint abstracts on concrete.

The old bent fists of trees
Throw knots of leaves
In the air.

A man digs.
Grass into earth
Into seed and unfolding leaf.

A cat
Chases the birds
Stalks round
Curls up in the sun.

The birds
Nesting in tree and gutter
Are freemen of all:
No tolls on their straw
No passports across their wall.

COMMUNITY

(Mr. Rogers, buried April 26, 1972)

There has been a death in the street.
Drawn curtains, collection for wreaths
The historians call it Cymortha,
Assume that it vanished
In the steam of industrial birth.

We're the size of a village: forty houses,
A shop. Over fences the women gossip,
Watch weddings and growings -observe
The proper and ritual tact
Of those who must live with their kin.

No blood ties, it's true; our bonds
Are accent and place -and desire
For much the same ends. We are not
Political animals; held
An Investiture feast for the children,

And praised all that pomp. On Sundays
Expediency pegs out the washing:
If God is not mocked -well, He knows us
I suppose it was like this before
When Piety lay in the clouds, an oncoming thunder.

There has been a death in the street:
We are less by that much. Statistics
Cannot say what we lose, what we give:
Questionnaires for the Welfare Department
Tell industrious lies.

We adapt. To the chimneys, the concrete,
The furnace, the smoke, the dead trees.
Our fields are the names of the roadways,
Our flocks and our language are gone:
But we hold our diminished city in face of the sun.

A DEATH IN LONDON, April 26th, 1972

i.
The minister,
Going by what he had heard,
Called it untimely death.

For those whom we love,
Knowing how much they contain,
All death is untimely.

ii.
After the funeral
We went back for a cup of tea:
In four hours nobody mentioned his name.

iii.
We cannot visit his grave,
And though we put Easter flowers,
His ghost has no resting place
But the troubled wind.

The grass is cut down and gone.
There is nothing left
But a name in a book
And a clock to be polished for love.

THE ANTIQUARIAN IN THE CONTRYSIDE

(Garreglwyd)

There are rhododendrons here too,
If not the same, similar
Enough to be confused.
There was also a lake,
A white house in the trees,
Soft voices along the pathway,
Mushroom umbrellas in the leaf-mould
Under a damp grey sky.

A proper setting for hermits,
For a Gothick folly, to live in
With a proper dispassionate joy.
In the village beyond
Lies Jerusalem, with a corrugated roof
And the Ten Commandments
Advising excess.

This is the same, not similar:
Trees, lake and castle
Seen in a composing mirror,
More elegant so.
Lawns, arbour and columns -
No tarnish on glass
The focus is out in the eye.

TEA WITH FRIENDS

This is 'commitment':
The spilled, sticky stain on the carpet,
The crying child
That use and exhaustion of time
Forbid to be comforted,
The careful, outfolding thought
That removes all roses to shelves too high to be seen.

This we would give each other:
For the silent moment
Alone; for the rhododendrons by the lake,
Grey stone and grey sky,
The quickening, pure conversation
Of I to myself.

This gift -whose price
We cannot be aware of
Till given; that is not revoked
After Christmas, like sweaters or socks
Whose makers were blinded by love:
False stitches, harsh colours, frayed edges,
These we accept with the gift.

It is not, after all, that perception is lost,
But the view
Is altered: the stain on the carpet
Is not to be judged from the lake.

HOUSEHOLD CAVALRY, LLANSTEFFAN

(For Dylan and Nesta)

We took the children down for an hour's outing,
Plenty of sun and sand and a good safe beach.
But there were the horses: perfect, bright shapes of wonder,
Tugging the stubborn grass with their vicious teeth.

Last night we had heard the music of their passage,
Drumming of hooves on the turf, the trumpeted air
Reeling at so much glory. Today we saw them
At ease in the picket lines on the littered Green.

Too much for the children; that majesty beyond them,
Something to know in a later year. They turned,
Exhausted, to mine the sand and build their castle,
A bulwark against the gentle tide's advance.

Soon, when the riders came, the horses altered;
No longer the distant princes, they plunged among us,
Raced in the shallow waves, set careless hoof marks
Flat on our broken fort, spurned shells and children.

Dangerous, yes; like lightning or flood or fire:
Something we could not contain, yet would not escape.
There on the warm safe sand the horses of anger
Already rode down the children as they played.

SUL Y BLODAU/PALM SUNDAY

You might call it the dead run.
A slow country bus trundling along the high road,
Disembarking at each chapel gate
Its cargo of flowers - flowers and women,
Each in her second-best jacket,
Prepared for the weather.

I, too. In my bag are the trowel,
Daffodils, paper, two jam jars;
I ride among beauty, these delicate trumpets of April.
It is almost a pastoral: sunlight, white clouds on blue oceans,
New buds on the branches, lambs leaping
The wind's knife at their throat in the sunshine.

And I too will descend,
Open the gate, find that corner
Where people unknown lie remembered;
Will harvest the weeds, wash the mud stains
Away from the stone, place new holders
In leaking memorial urns.

Earth under my nails, feet half frozen,
I wedge fallen jars with the chippings
Against the wind's malice; feel pity
For beauty that dies - that I slaughter
By offering here its frail gold.

Later, on the bus, I ride homeward
Past clumps of cold fire;
Note a patchwork of meetings, conversations
Of annual strangers. It seems
A curious, silent beginning
Beneath the sharp rain.

MISCARRIAGE

I lie at the top of the stairs,
Feeling the blood pump out.
The doctor, hastily summoned,
Hovers in nervous concern.
"The ambulance -
They'll be here at once,
We'll save the child, truly -"
But I know it has gone,
Have known it for days.
A maimed thing at best
I pray in my heart
That they'll reach me too late.

When they come, all is action.
The ambulance blaring its note
Through the dangerous rush-to-work traffic.
I clench nerves like tight fists,
Holding on to my life ...
And at home you tidy the landing,
Mop up the spilt blood,
Comfort the children

I never ask
What else you cleaned up;
If the parcel of papers
Held the girl-child you'd hoped for.
We meet in a union of silence:
Each of us coping alone
For the other's loss.

AFTER THE PASSION PLAY

I am not a religious man, says Father Kearney.
Jesus is queuing with Caiaphas for a buffet snack,
And the First Priest, pocketing Caesar's head,
Asks for a quid for some fags.

Under the serious gaze of the Little Flower
The people of Jerusalem are indulging themselves
In an orgy of sausages and squash; an exhausted child
Has tumbled to sleep among trestles and paper cloths.

Earlier, out in the park, we howled for blood
Were mostly aware of the damp and the stinging flies
And the need to avoid the Temple Guards (whose spears
Were rather too sharp for comfort) as we fled.

It was not a religious play; what we remember
Has nothing to do with piety. Instead,
The crush in the parish hall, the makeup sponge
Converting us all to pilgrims, then the stones

Clattering underfoot, imitation palms
Shrinking each day as the bamboo grove was stripped
And each day, at the end, the white figure under the trees,
Alone in the gathering dusk - the incredible words.

I am not a religious man, says Father Kearney.
Politely, we laugh -but all of us here could say it.
Also, no doubt, the carpenter's son, who himself
Was aware of the need for a proper disrespect.

THE APPRENTICE ARTIST

'Make me a house -'
And so geometrical love
Marks out the square frame,
The triangle roof, the windows
Precisely arranged
Round the oblong that serves as a door.

'Make me a house,'
And beyond the brisk pattern of duty
Are grace notes of flowers,
A tree, curling smoke from the chimneys,
A child looking out.

And later I found a white shower
Of copied mansions:
Exact to the smallest waver
In wall or hedgerow.
Yet each with its own bold selfhood:
An enormous 3

** *

All over the house there are pictures.
Like a berserk da Vinci
He draws on the back of doors,
Throttles the chairs and tables
In coccoons of sellotaped colour.
We are adrift on a sea of paper,
Drowning in faces
Flat, yet alive - a demoniac caveman,
He brings nightmares to life
With a vigour I cannot encompass,
Leaves all the house haunted
With desires just beyond his expressing.

PASSING ACQUAINTANCE, PONTRHYDYFEN

"What's your name ?" he asked.
I offered invisible sweets
And he munched them loudly.

Flashing lights on the upper road:
"Oh look, there's an ambulance -
Pity whoever's inside it -
He likes ambulances," his mother told me.

"Fire engines I like," said the boy.
"Have you got a sandwich ?"
Rain dripped in a steady dampness
As we watched the traffic
And he chewed on the watery air.

I offered him cherry cake;
Invisible fruit in my hand
But he wanted stories.

"I'll tell you about this dragon ... "
"I want Three Bears first,
Goldilocks and her porridge."

In the bus, writing his name on the window,
He sang 'Gee Ceffyl Bach';
Outside a river was rising.

Soon I got off; abandoned already.
His fingers traced shapes in the water,
A world all his own.

A STONE FOR REMEMBRANCE

*(Dedication of the memorial to the crew of the Mumbles
lifeboat, Sker Point, 1992)*

Smooth, perfect, complete;
A curious memorial of that shattered moment
When ship and lives together splintered on the stones.
Curious, too, this ghost of a ship that rides
Silent, unmanned, a stone's throw from the shore,
Patrolling the vigorous waves.

'For those in peril on the sea' we sing
While the restless tide
Grinds pebbles and lives underfoot,
And the buffeting wind
Tears at our wavering voices
In the clear, sharp light.

ENROLMENT EVENING

All these eager seekers after enlightenment:
Jolly middle-aged ladies, mostly with friends,
House-husbands wanting a moment away from the stove,
Young wives trying not to succumb to the gut-call of nappies,
A few rebels discreetly conforming.

Once they'd have channelled this fervour
Into black-leading grates
Or polishing doorsteps or brass.
(And we still half-expect the domestic:
In this room where we sit,
Sink units and cookers,
The blurred glass of a kitchen extension.)

Once all these skills
Would have come as a part of the pattern
Learnt every day:
Those gracenotes of life that made bearable
So much contempt.

Not great art, but a honing of minds
That brings greatness in reach.

LOSS

'What is a black hole ?'
Asks the child on the train.

This, I could tell her, this -
This nothingness that cannot be filled,
This bottomless unknown,
This hole in the world ...

Those phrases, so grandly dramatic,
So much less than the truth.

CORSHAM COURT GARDENS 1993

Minerva's owls sit erect
Alert for the kill.
Above them the chestnut candles
Blaze into summer, and wisteria
Hangs, elegantly, over the wall.
A peopled stillness, a silence
Full of birdsong and distant movement;
Dark green of the yew-tree branches
Bows deeply; slow-motion wind
Stirs them to dancing shadows.

But the wind is still cold,
Summer a frosty illusion.
Minerva's owls
Are ice in the mossy shadows,
Dead to the touch.

RANDOM THOUGHTS OF A FALLEN WOMAN IN BUTE STREET

This pavement is clean - but badly composed.
I admire the mica sheen in its coarse-grained slabs
And the elegant overhang where my face met the road.

It is pleasant down here: not raining.
Relaxed, I consider the future:
No doubt a damage report will surface in time
But till then I'm content.

Yet this is a moral decline - a dialectical pit
Into which I plunged headlong. Observing the skies,
I failed to observe the earth, was brought low
By a summons to heaven. As I lie,
I consider the pattern of life in the dust - observe
A strayed carrot cartwheel in slipstream.

Time disappeared
As I toppled; was suspended, extended ... who knows ?
I could lie here for ever, unnoticed,
Compose volumes, speculations, a whole mythos
From granite and space.

But time recommences. A hand
Reaches out and a voice asks if I
Am 'all right' ? Can I manage ?'
'Of course,' I reply,
Heaving up from the dust.
Contemplation is over. I limp
Towards new revelations elsewhere.

HAWEN WARD, THE INFIRMARY

'Any news ?'

But there isn't any, of course.
Only the things we said last Thursday
And before that on Sunday, Saturday, Thursday,
The Sunday before that
A tedious procession of nothings.

Outside I noticed a primrose
Knotted among the straw;
The river is full,
There's snow on the distant hills.
I try to parcel them up
As an extra gift
Along with the tissues and squash
And the magazines.

But I doubt if she hears me.
There are too many sounds in the room,
And soon she is cross,
Frustrated and sleepy.
I know it is time to go.

On the way to the station
I shiver.
No air-conditioning here,
No sanitised calm.
Out here the world moves along,
Hot or cold, untidy and painful.
There is always news.

THE AUTHOR ADMITS GUILT

Paper is taking over.
Newspaper, wallpaper, paper
For mopping up milk.
Paper disintegrating,
Peeling off walls
Damp with the sweat of bad weather.
Everywhere paper.

Paper becomes an addiction:
A little pad
Tucked into one's pocket,
A novel
(Paperback, of course)
Lurking inside one's handbag,
The hasty fix
Snatched between bed and breakfast.

Paper of every colour,
Of every pattern -
Delicate flowers on water,
Adverts, junk mail -
But there, after all, at the end,
The paper that haunts our silence:
White pages we rape.

BOOKLAUNCH, SOUTHAMPTON ROW

Thirty years ago perhaps I knew these faces.
Now there's familiarity (also perhaps) but I cannot be sure ...
They cluster in stockbroker clumps and discuss ... ?

I cannot imagine ...
Even their rebels are sedate,
Clean-faced in their grey anoraks.

Two young ladies, supplied by the publisher,
Are polite and encouraging and offer me canapes.
It is all very cultured.

Why did I come here ? I wonder;
Remnant of the Sixties, dredged up for this paper survival.
I have nothing in common with them
The world has moved on ... and I with it.
Later I purchase a copy and withdraw.

BINGO

By now I can manage two cards:
Twenty pennorth of riotous living.
I steady my pen and wait for the caller to start.
'Eighty and two, eighty-two. On its own, number one -'
My eye flicks over the rows, marks off the squares.
It's a good night tonight, only two and I've finished a line -
But too late, someone else is before me.
Then, almost a house - but almost is nowhere.
Next time, perhaps - but I feel in my nerves
The beat of the gambler's rush.

It is time.
Salvation arrives with the bus.

SCARS

Like any old soldier I bear my scars.
This here, on the wrist, where the iron swung,
Spittle still hissing on metal,
And burned its mark;
This other, where, cutting an apple,
The knife sliced in
Reminding me now of fifty years ago,
Gold light in the garden,
Roses and phlox, and the grass
Burning to brown in the sunshine.
Or this neat horseshoe
Trimmed at the Swallow Falls
When a careless foot
Slid on the muddy stone.
But you shaped me more than all these
And of your work
There is nothing to see.
Only an absence of pain.

WAITING FOR THE FUNERAL TO ARRIVE

Someone I have never known,
Though I wrote to her monthly:
"Sunday services in May ...
Thanksgiving for harvest on the tenth ...
Mrs. Davies has not been well ....
The Sisterhood meets each Monday ... "
Did she ever read them, I wonder ?
Was she aware that we remembered ?
Or does somewhere a dusty pyramid
Lie in an empty hall ?

Already our lives have moved on.
The sun still shines, a light breeze
Ruffles my hair,
Somewhere an organ plays, rehearsing farewell.
Coming by bus, I am early;
Soon the dark cars will arrive,
The chapel will fill, the service fulfil its purpose,
She'll be committed to what comes next
(Whatever that is)
Like a traveller catching the train.
And once it has gone
We'll disperse with the usual chatter
Who's here, who is not,
How correctly the minister spoke.
(Whistling against the dark - the young have no time to be here,
And briefly we see ourselves in that central role.)

There's a purpose, of course; the serious moment
Of condolence,
Our presence a measure of worth.
But also, for us, a reminder of what we still have;
Voices we hear, hands that we touch, the bright sky
Arching from mountain to harbour - and the stain
Seeping away from the furnace.
Unlike her, we have not reached perfection
Perhaps never will ?

FOUND POEM

(Cork City Library, Saturday, September 5th, 1998)

"It is earnestly requested that readers use the books with care;
Do not, if you please, soil them, or cut, or tear,
Do not turn down their leaves, or write in them or, indeed,
Make any marks on them at all, or wet them with dragging thumbs
This should be especially avoided.
Any injury to books will be dealt with
As the Rules and the Byelaws provide."

Now this is a proper respect for the lifeblood of nations;
Mind speaking to mind over centuries, continents, worlds.
At home our new library clicks with the song of computers.
The Chair of the Library Committee beams at the glorious sight.
"I look forward," he says, "to the time when we're fully updated:
When there's no longer a need
For these shelves of untidy books."

FLOOD DAMAGE

It was metrication that caused it.
Such a narrow fraction -
But water will creep anywhere,
Oozing between the threads.

The cold, bronze-coloured tap
Was helpless against that invasion,
And under the sink the bucket
Soon brimmed with soapsuds.

Arm muscles grew strong
As I balanced the heavy pail
Out to the drain,
Counterweighting our future.
And elsewhere the bright silver traces
Infiltrated our fortress;
Floorboards weakened,
Wallpaper stained and a ceiling
Dropped casually down.

After that we took steps.
Rotted wood gave way to cold concrete.

Now our ship's battened tight,
Sailing through storms and bad plumbing
With no hint of a leak.

Yet sometimes I almost regret them,
Those watery days:
Watching the slow permeation
Of plaster and wood,
Damp patterns on paper,
Complex and strange ...
Water is life, shaping us
Undermining our plans.

FRIENDS OF MARGAM PARK

Easter Monday, 5.4.99

A grey day, of course. The mist, rising slowly,
Conceals a watery sun,
The rough stones of the abbey shiver,
Alone in the chill of the park.
Plant stalls and face-painting,
The usual home-made cakes;
The mortar of conservation,
Holding history together.

We sip strong tea delicately
Where tea-party George looks down
In a faded glamour of ermine.
Beyond the door an Easter clown explains
The rules of the egg-hunt
And two well-dressed rabbits
Saunter among mannikin children.

It would be easy to imagine echoes.
An ethereal chanting
From the Chapter House over the way
Or a periwigged huntsman inspecting his orange trees.

But this is today.
Anoraks and trainers
Infants in push-chairs,
Clowns,
Usurp the mastery now.
And the last of the castle's ghosts
Hovers lightly above painted children,
A butterfly smile on her face.

BIG ISSUE

'I only had forty today, and they're all gone,' she told me.
'And this man brought me some blankets.'
Bright yellow, like my own.

I totted it up.
Forty at fifty pence is twenty pounds
Which is what I have. And sometimes better ?
And sometimes worse.
The weather today is passable, today she met
Someone with yellow blankets - and today she has
A sore on her face, and beyond her smile a hunger
For somewhere that is her own ...
Without that she does not exist,
Is marginal to the equation.

And in the day centre someone complains
That these vagrants litter the streets
She too on the margin.

PALM SATURDAY/SADWRN Y BLODAU

Peace March, Whitehall, April 12, 2003

This year too there are flowers.
Flowers for those with no graves.
We throw them across the barrier
In front of the watching guards:
A single rose, a cluster of daffodils
A teddy bear ...
This year there will be no young men
Bulldozed into the sand.
Only children
In pain in a looted ward,
A family dead in their car
Because someone's afraid.
Two languages and no translator.

And here, so far from that battleground,
We fight their war too
With roses and toys,
With drums and banners and horns ...
Tomorrow it will happen again,
The ride to Jerusalem,
The splendour that leads to Gethsemane:
The tomb in the garden.

YUGOSLAVIA 1982

I have two gifts from Macedonia:
The first picked by my grandfather for his young daughter,
Prayer book and Bible, both neatly inscribed
'Salonica 1917'.
They have survived move after move,
Death after death,
Hard words and hard weather.
Rest now,
In the chaos of a life seeking order:
Offer charity and peace.

Nearby on the shelf are two flutes,
Carved wood, brightly painted.

Mementoes, this time, of our friendship,
Of the evening we sat, without labels,
And talked in the twilight together,
Sharing music and wine.

AT THE DYLAN THOMAS CENTRE

'Was it a special birthday ?' she asks.
'Seventy,' I say -and halt, astonished.
Can I be that ?

It never *is* that, I know it,
Whatever our bones may suggest.
Inside we are all just twenty,
Our lives and our dreams ahead.

Of course, we begin to consider
What's needed, what's not,
That much is our debt to their future -
But ours is not gone. On that day
I stood on my brother's terrace
And looked outward, to Africa.

Acknowledgements

Some of these poems have appeared previously in *Turning Away* (Gomer Press, 1969), *The Forgotten Country* (Gomer Press, 1977) and *Relative Values* (Poetry Wales Press, 1985).

Others have appeared in anthologies and magazines including *Poetry Review*, *Poetry Wales*, the *Anglo-Welsh Review*, *Swagmag*, *Roundyhouse*, and *Over Milk Woood*, *Poetry '69* and *Poetry '76*.

Sally Roberts Jones

Notes for a Life is Sally Roberts Jones' fifth collection of poems. She is also a biographer, critic, historian and bibliographer. She read History at the University College of North Wales, Bangor, worked as a librarian in Greater London in the Sixties and moved to South Wales in 1967 and lives there still, in Port Talbot. She was a founder member of the Welsh Academy (English language section) in 1968, and its Secretary and Treasurer from 1968-75, and Chair from 1993-97. Sally has written and lectured on the cultural and industrial history of Wales, as well as publishing poetry, verse plays and children's stories for radio. She has run workshops and courses for schools and adults and was a Royal Literary Fund Fellow at Swansea University, 1999-2001 and 2004-2009, Associate Fellow 2001-2002, also Project Fellow 2002-2004 on the Afan Valley Project in Glamorgan, based in local libraries.

Sally is on the Editorial Board of Roundyhouse Poetry Magazine and runs the small press, Alun Books, which she founded with her late husband, Alwyn Jones.